*The Book*

# Logan of Love

# Table of contents

The Book
  Introduction
  Chapter One
  DoodleNotes
  Chapter Two
  DoodleNotes
  Chapter Three
  DoodleaNotes
  Chapter Four
  DoodleNotes
  Chapter Five
  DoodleNotes
  Activation Break
  Chapter Six
  DoodleNotes
  Chapter Seven
  DoodleNotes
  Chapter Eight
  DoodleNotes
  Chapter Nine
  DoodleNotes
  Unfuck Your Fuck
  Chapter Ten
  DoodleNotes
  Chapter Eleven
  DoodleNotes
  Chapter Twelve

DoodleNotes
Chapter Thirteen
A Sprinkle of Stardust & Shenanigans
With Love, Laughter & Cosmic Gratitude
A Little Thank You

# The Book

You didn't get a manual at birth…. this is it.
Part truth scroll, part spiritual slap, The Book is for the wild, glitchy souls waking up in a world that doesn't make sense.

You're not broken.
You're buffering.
This is your upgrade.

# Introduction

Welcome, wild soul.
If you've found yourself here, this isn't an accident. The Universe doesn't do "oops." You were summoned.

You, with your messy magic and your fire that won't go out.
You, with your tired heart that still dares to Love.
You, the truth-seeker, the illusion-breaker, the one who always knew there was something more.

This is your permission slip to be wildly yourself. To cackle at the chaos. To say fuck it to what doesn't serve you. To stop overcomplicating what your soul has known all along.

This book is not going to tell you to eat more kale, align your chakras at the exact hour of Mercury retrograde, or burn your ex's hoodie in a ceremonial blaze of closure. Nope. This book is different.

This book.
Is a rebellion.
A sacred scroll.
A slap and a cuddle.
A cosmic map scribbled on the back of a napkin with glitter pen and a bit of tea spilled on it.

You've been navigating Earth School the hard way.
This book? It's your permission slip to stop pretending you don't know the answers because you do.
You've just been distracted by the noise, the shame, the "shoulds" and the spiritual fluff that smells more like profit than purpose.

Inside these chapters, we're cutting through the crap.
This is grounded truth, delivered with Love, humour, and absolutely zero sugar-coating.
You'll get cheeky lessons, cosmic nudges, and potent reminders that you are and have always been the damn magic.

Each page is a cheat code.
Each scroll a spark of remembering.
Each chapter is a key you already hold, but forgot how to use.

So breathe in.
Exhale the performance.
Shake off the guilt.
Take my hand and let's begin.

Because the truth is you've never been too much.
You've just been reading from the wrong script.

Until now. Let the remembering begin.
Let the truth rise.
Let the bullshit burn.

Love,
Logan of Love

## Chapter One

Welcome, You Glorious Chaos Magnet

The Note You Were Supposed to Get at Birth… But Didn't

You incarnated during rush hour in the Universe. They forgot your welcome pack. There was supposed to be a sparkly scroll, a cosmic pep talk, and maybe even some confetti. Instead, you got noise, pressure, trauma, and bills.

And still… here you are. Glorious.
A walking contradiction of soul and sass.
A divine being shoved into a meat suit with a nervous system designed for lions, not emails and existential dread.

Let's stop pretending this is normal. It's not. It's bananas.

 Chaos is Not a Problem. It's a Signal.

You're not a mess, you're a magnet.
To experiences.
To lessons.
To people who can't help but be drawn to your energy… then freak out because they see themselves too clearly in your mirror.

The chaos you've lived through?
That wasn't punishment.
It was preparation.

You were never meant to be mild.
You were built for depth.
For Love. For truth. For unraveling what no one else wants to look

at.

## ⚡ Why You're So Tired All The Time

No, it's not just your iron levels.
It's because you've been holding everything together for everyone for way too long.

You're the safe space.

The feeler.

The fixer.

The one who says "I'm fine" when your soul is literally screaming into a pillow made of moonlight and rage.

And somewhere along the line, you started to believe that being strong meant staying quiet.

Let's end that narrative.
Let's burn that script.
Let's start **again**... with truth.

Truth Moment:

The Universe didn't put you here to:

Play small

Be polite while your soul rots

Apologise for your sensitivity

Explain your weirdness like it's a malfunction

You are not a glitch.
You're the damn upgrade.
What's Actually Going On

You're waking up.
You're glitching because the old code isn't working anymore.

You can't un-know what you've felt.
You can't re-bury what your soul's already dug up.

And that's terrifying.
Because real awakening doesn't feel like unicorns and incense.
It feels like ripping wallpaper off your entire reality.. by hand.
Half-blind. Crying. Still showing up for work.

But on the other side of the ripping?
Freedom.
Peace.
Clarity.
Joy that doesn't feel like it might explode if you breathe too loud.

## THE CHEAT CODE

You're not broken. You're buffering.

The loading symbol you feel spinning inside your chest? That's your soul trying to update the system while your ego screams, "Am I dying or is this just a spiritual awakening!?"

You are allowed to pause.
You are allowed to not know.
You are allowed to rest while the download completes.

Your New Reality Starts Here:

Repeat after me (loud, like the badass you are):

I'm not a problem to be fixed.

I am power in a human disguise.

I am Love learning to take up space.

I honour the chaos, because it's my teacher.

And I no longer shrink to make others feel safe.

So welcome, wild one.
You glorious, glitchy, galaxy-hearted human.
You're not here to be perfect.
You're here to remember who the fuck you are.

Let's get you logged in properly.
Next stop: The Matrix... Bring snacks.

Scroll from the Universe:

Found at the foot of your soul the day you were born... but misplaced in the chaos of Earth.

To the One Who Feels Too Much,
Thinks Too Deeply,
And Still Shows Up Anyway...

You were never meant to blend in.
You were carved from stars and wrapped in skin,
Dropped into madness not to be consumed by it,
But to re-code it.

When you cry — you cleanse timelines.
When you laugh — you shatter illusions.
When you rest — the Earth exhales.
When you rise — shadows tremble.

You are not "too much."
You are the exact amount needed to shift everything.

So stop waiting for permission.
Stop shrinking in the name of peace.
Stop explaining your fire to those who fear heat.

You are the prophecy they never saw coming.
The storm with soft hands.
The spell with a heartbeat.
The Love that remembers.

Signed,
The Universe (and your higher self)

○ Take a breath.
○ Notice what's stirring.
○ No need to fix it. Just feel it.

# *Doodle Notes*

## Your Sacred Space

## Chapter Two

The Matrix is Real... and You're in It

(But don't worry... you're also the damn Glitch)

Let's get this out of the way early:

If life feels rigged, it's because parts of it are.
But guess what? You're not here to follow the program...
You're here to bend it. Twist it. Maybe even chuck the whole system into a black hole and build your own.

☐ Welcome to Earth:

You arrive here, fresh from the stars, wide-eyed and electric...
Then BOOM!... the programming begins:

"Be a good girl/boy."

"Sit still."

"Don't cry."

"That's just the way things are."

"You can't just follow your dreams... be realistic!"

"Here, have anxiety. We all do."

"Get a mortgage and try not to die inside."

And like any good system, it rewards you for compliance and punishes you for questioning.

You were taught to:

Doubt your gut

Ignore your inner nudges

Trust people in suits more than your own soul

And you started believing them. Because you had to survive.

The Red Pill Moment

You ever notice how weird it is to be alive right now?
People are out here paying for bottled water while scrolling through doom, worrying about being "too much" while drinking caffeine to mask exhaustion and calling that balance.

That glitch in the gut feeling?
That whisper that says, "Something's off…"
That's your soul trying to wake you up.

You don't belong to the matrix.
You're the anomaly it couldn't predict.

Programming You Didn't Ask For:

Let's call it out:

Consumerism: Buy your worth. More stuff = more value.

Perfectionism: Be flawless or be forgotten.

People-Pleasing: Earn your place by shrinking.

Fear-Based Reality: The world is unsafe. Better stay small.

Hustle Culture: If you're not exhausted, you're not doing enough.

All of this was sold to you as "truth."
But it's just dusty old code.

Cheat Code Alert:
If the program makes you betray your soul, it's a virus … not a

value.

## What Happens When You Glitch

When you start saying:

"I'm not available for that anymore."

"That doesn't sit right with me."

"I don't care what's normal… I want what's real."

"I'm done playing small just to be liked."

THE SYSTEM. WILL. SHAKE.

People might ghost you.
Your old life might crumble.
You might even feel like you're falling apart.

But baby, you're not falling apart… you're unplugging.
And yes, it's scary as hell.
But freedom always is at first.

## So… What Do You Do With This Truth?

You get intentional.
You question everything.
You stop waiting for external validation like a dog begging for treats.
You take radical responsibility for your energy.
You own your story… even the messy, WTF chapters.

The Real Secret?

The Matrix isn't just the outside world.

It's your thoughts.
Your beliefs.
Your inherited patterns.
The voice in your head that tells you you're "too much" or "not

enough."

That voice? That's not you. That's the programming.

And you can rewrite it.

CHEAT CODE:

Just because it's "normal"
doesn't mean it's not fucked.

"Normal" is a setting on the washing machine, not a goal for your life.
Rebel, rewire, and reclaim what's true for you.

Scroll from the Universe:

Discovered in your sock drawer next to the crystals and unpaid bills

Dear Soul Hacker,

You were never meant to download the full illusion.
You came encoded with truth.
You came remembering what others forgot.

If the system makes you numb, question it.
If the people say "you've changed," say "thank you."
If your intuition contradicts the rules...
burn the rules.

You are not here to survive the matrix.
You are here to dismantle it
with Love, with fire,
and a sparkle in your eye that says:

"I remember who I am."

Signed,
The Universe (via your rebellious higher self)

Pause. Exhale. Check your code.

What beliefs am I running on autopilot?
Whose rules am I still obeying without question?
Where do I feel the "ick"… but keep going anyway?

Tiny truth bomb: Awareness is your first rebellion.
You don't have to fix it all right now. Just notice.

# DoodleNotes
## Your Sacred Space

## Chapter Three

Feelings Are Wi-Fi Signals, Not Traffic Lights

(So stop parking in sadness and calling it "being stuck")

Let's start with a cosmic truth that'll rattle your root chakra:

Your feelings aren't problems.
They're bloody portals.

But most of us were raised on the emotional equivalent of dial-up. Slow to load, full of screeching, and everyone in the house told you to shut it off before it ruined everything.

The Programming: Emotional Edition

Remember this?

"Stop crying, you're fine."

"Be strong."

"Don't get angry, that's not nice."

"You're too sensitive."

"Don't let your emotions control you."

Translation:
"Hide the parts of you that make me uncomfortable."

So we learned to:

Numb

Suppress

Laugh through pain

Meditate away rage

And scroll past our sadness with motivational quotes and oat milk lattes and herbal teas 🫖☕

But the truth?

Your emotions are data, not danger.
They're sacred. They're electric. They're messengers, not enemies.

⚡ What Your Emotions Are REALLY Saying

Let's decode the emotional Wi-Fi for a sec:

Anger = Something sacred in you was violated. Act.

Sadness = You're grieving something real. Be still.

Joy = You're in alignment. Keep going.

Fear = Look deeper. Protection or illusion?

Anxiety = You're living in a timeline that hasn't happened yet.

Guilt = Check your integrity, not your worth.

Numbness = Your soul is buffering again, babe. You need space.

The "Low Vibe" Lie

In spiritual circles, people will shame you for feeling "low vibe."
As if being human is a vibe crime.

But real talk?

"High vibe only" is emotional gentrification.
Healing includes rage, grief, shadow, snot, and days where you stare at the wall like a haunted potato.

There is no emotion that makes you less spiritual.
You're not failing because you're feeling.

You're feeling because you're healing.

Feel It... Don't Move In

Here's the catch:
Feelings are visitors. Not squatters.

The problem isn't the emotion...
it's when you build a shrine to it, write poetry about your pain but never release it, or let your sadness drive the car with fear on the aux cable playing sad girl anthems on loop.

You're allowed to feel it all.
But you're not meant to become it all.

Hold it. Hear it. Then let it move.

Emotions are energy in motion (literally: e-motion).
And baby, when you trap that energy, you're just bottling lightning with a tight jaw and chronic back pain.

How to Actually Feel Your Feelings (Without Exploding)

1. Name It: "I feel…" Not "I am…"

2. Notice Where It Lives: Throat? Chest? Belly?

3. Breathe Into It: No fixing. Just witnessing.

4. Ask It What It Needs: Movement? Silence? Screaming into a pillow shaped like your ex?

5. Let It Move: Walk. Dance. Cry. Shake. Yell into a mountain.

6. Release Judgment: Feelings aren't moral. They're messengers.

CHEAT CODE:

"Low vibe" doesn't mean "wrong vibe."

Your feelings are a fucking superpower.
Stop apologising for being tuned in.

Scroll from the Universe:

Found rolled inside your pillowcase after a breakdown and a really good cry.

Dearest Feel-Everything Soul,

You weren't made to be numb.
You are a symphony of sensation,
A storm in soft skin,
A translator of energy in a world afraid of depth.

Don't shame your tears...
they are holy rivers.
Don't fear your fire...
it's ancient medicine.

Every feeling you've ever buried
was a sacred telegram.
This is your permission slip
to start reading them.

You are not "too emotional."
You are a fucking antenna for truth.

Signed,
The Universe (and your nervous system's biggest fan)

You just downloaded some sacred truth.
Let's take a pause before your nervous system crashes like a retro dial-up modem.

Ask yourself:
- What emotion have I been parking in lately?
- Have I been feeling it… or becoming it?
- Where in my body is that signal trying to get through?

Reminder:
You don't need to fix your feelings.
You just need to feel them without fear.

Sit with them. Listen. Let the energy move.
That's not breakdown energy…. it's breakthrough power.

## Your Sacred Space

## Chapter Four

Manifestation Is Not Ordering a Pizza

(The Law of Attraction, Demystified and De-fluffed)

You've heard it all before, haven't you?

"Just think positive!"
"Raise your vibration!"
"Ask, believe, receive!"
"Visualise it and it's yours!"

And the most brutal one:
"If it's not happening, you're doing it wrong." 

Meanwhile, you're sitting on your bedroom floor, surrounded by candles, moon water, and a half-written gratitude list wondering why the hell your dream hasn't shown up yet.

Here's the truth:
Manifestation is not Deliveroo for your desires.

You don't just "order abundance" and expect it to be delivered hot and fresh in 30 minutes or less.

The Cosmic Customer Service Myth

You were sold the idea that manifestation is like an app:

1. Place order (aka set intention)

2. Be positive while you wait

3. Voilà, new job, soulmate, dream house arrives

4. If it doesn't? "It wasn't aligned" or "Your vibe was off"

But let's be real.

Manifestation isn't passive.
It's alchemy.

It's part mindset, part embodiment, part divine timing, and part "Holy shit, this is gonna make me confront my deepest wounds before it arrives."

Why It Feels Like Nothing's Happening

Sometimes when you ask for "more Love," the Universe doesn't send a partner...
it sends every part of you that's still afraid to receive it.

You want money?
You might get shown all your scarcity wounds first.

Want confidence?

Here comes a situation to test everything that ever made you doubt yourself.

Because the Universe doesn't give you what you ask for.
It gives you the opportunities to become who can hold it.

Oof. Yep.

Deep breaths, lovebug.

Manifestation ≠ Avoiding Reality

Real manifestation isn't about sitting in lotus pose pretending you're a millionaire while your bank account sobs.

It's about:

Facing your fear without becoming it

Walking your truth before it's popular

Acting like the person you're becoming… even when you're sweating and shaking

You don't get the dream by waiting.
You get it by becoming the version of you who already lives it.

Here's What Actually Works:

1. CLARITY — What do you really want? Not what you think you should want.

2. BELIEF — Do you actually believe it's possible… for YOU?

3. ACTION — Are your choices matching your vision?

4. RECEIVING — Can you hold the thing you say you want without sabotaging it?

5. DETACHMENT — Can you let go and trust… while still showing

up?

It's not about controlling the outcome.
It's about dancing with it.
Tuning into its frequency without needing it to arrive on your timeline.
Manifestation Red Flags (That No One Talks About):

Bypassing your current pain by pretending you're "already there"
Obsessing over every detail like the Universe is a waiter you're about to yell at
Judging yourself for having doubts — and trying to "vibe" your way out of them
Blaming yourself when it doesn't show up instantly
Using crystals as wish tokens instead of energy allies


CHEAT CODE:

Energy flows where your embodiment goes.
You don't attract what you want.
You attract what you believe you are allowed to receive.


Mic. Drop.



Scroll from the Universe:

Found hidden inside your Pinterest board, disguised as a glittery quote.

Dear Cosmic Co-Creator,

You were never meant to sit and wait.
You were meant to move like it's already yours.

You were meant to open your palms and let the sacred chaos of becoming crack you wide open.

This is not about asking once and hoping.
It's about asking boldly,
becoming bravely,
and trusting wildly.

You are not "doing it wrong."
You are unlearning every lie that told you you weren't worthy of receiving.

Keep becoming.
Keep becoming.
Keep becoming.

Signed,
The Universe (your ride-or-die manifesting partner)

"You're Not Waiting for It… You're Becoming It"

Your Manifestation Integration Moment:

Describe your current desire as if it's already here.
"I am living in a reality where…"
Let it flow like you already feel it in your bones.

What belief do you secretly hold that might be blocking it?
Dig deep. Is it fear of not being good enough? Fear of it being taken away? Write it down. Get honest.

Choose a baby action that matches your desire today.
Just one. Book the class. Say the "no." Wear the outfit. Speak your truth. Be the you who already has it.

4. Write this affirmation 3x like a manifesting spell:
"I am becoming the version of me who knows I am worthy of receiving."

5. Sit still for one minute. Breathe. Then ask:
"What part of me still thinks I have to hustle to earn what's meant for me?"

Journal what comes up. Let that version of you be seen... then gently show them a better way.

## DoodleNotes
### Your Sacred Space

# Chapter Five

Boundaries Aren't Mean… They're Magic
(No is a full sentence. And a Love spell.)
Let's begin with a hard truth wrapped in glitter:
If you're constantly drained, anxious, or resentful, you don't have an energy problem… you have a boundary problem.
And you're not alone. Most of us were raised on "be nice" culture. Especially if you're empathetic, sensitive, spiritual, or raised to make others comfortable no matter how much it costs you.
But here's the thing: Self-abandonment in the name of kindness isn't noble… it's self-harm with a halo. 🌀

The Programming That Broke Your Boundaries
Somewhere along the line, you were taught:
Saying "no" is rude
You must explain yourself to be valid
Putting yourself first is selfish
Forgiveness means letting them stay
You're responsible for how others feel
Bull. Shit. You are not here to be a 24/7 emotional sponge in a world of leaky faucets.

What Boundaries Really Are
Let's clear this up right now:
Boundaries are not walls. They're doors with locks… that YOU control.
They say:
"This is my energy. You don't get to siphon it."
"This is my time. I choose how I spend it."
"This is my heart. You don't get to trample it and call it love."
Boundaries don't push people away. They protect the connection

you have with yourself.
And when you honour that? You attract people who do, too.
Without Boundaries, You'll…
Resent the people you keep saying yes to
Burn out from carrying what isn't yours
Second-guess yourself constantly
Say "it's fine" while silently screaming inside
Turn into a people-pleasing husk with sage smoke in your eyes and no idea where your joy went
Say it With Me:
"I am not responsible for other people's reactions to my truth."
Say it louder. Say it at the family dinner table. Say it to the ghost of your people-pleasing past. 🫠
Because truth without boundaries is a song with no rhythm. It's chaos masquerading as compassion.

How to Start Building Boundaries (Even If You've Never Had Any)

Get Clear: What are your non-negotiables? What leaves you feeling drained vs energised?

Use Simple Language: "No." "That doesn't work for me." "I'm not available for that."

Ditch the Guilt: You're not "bad" for protecting yourself. That's survival and self-Love.

Enforce Without Explaining: If someone asks "Why?" you don't owe a TED Talk.

Hold the Line: The first time you set a boundary, people will test it. That doesn't mean it's wrong. That means it's working.

Boundaries Are Energy Magic
Think of them like spiritual filters. When you hold your line, you only allow in what resonates with your truth.
A boundary is you choosing to honour yourself in a world that profits from your self-abandonment.
You can be kind AND firm. Soft AND sovereign. Empathic AND unavailable for nonsense.

CHEAT CODE:
Your peace is your job. Protect it like it's sacred... because it is.
Scroll from the Universe:
Found tucked under your doormat after you ghosted someone with toxic vibes.
Dear Sacred Soul with a Spine,
You were never meant to be endlessly available. You were meant to choose. To discern. To curate your connections like altars.
Every "no" you say in truth is a "yes" to your healing. Every line you draw in Love becomes a shield of protection.
Boundaries don't make you harsh. They make you holy.
Protect your energy like the treasure it is. The right ones will honour the gate. The rest can vibe elsewhere.
Signed, The Universe (and your finally-activated solar plexus)

"Boundaries Aren't Walls... They're Self-Love in Action"

Energetic Audit & Boundary Spellbook:

1. List 3 things currently draining your energy
Ask yourself: "Why am I still saying yes to this?"

2. Complete this boundary spell:
"From this moment on, I give myself full permission to say NO to..."

3. Circle one sacred YES you've been denying yourself out of guilt or fear
Now, plan how to honour it this week. (Yes, even if it's a nap.)

4. Draw a line (literally or mentally):
"This is the line. I honour it. I protect it. I don't cross it for anyone... not even the old version of me."

5. Mirror Magic Affirmation:
"My boundaries aren't cruelty. They're clarity. And I am crystal clear on what I deserve."

Shadow Work Bonus Prompt:
What part of you still believes that Love = overgiving?
Whisper to them gently, then remind them who's in charge now (hint: it's you, beautiful).

## Doodle Notes

**Your Sacred Space**

# Activation Break

"The Code in My Bones Poem"

I was born with a map in my marrow,
A blueprint scribbled in stardust and borrowed
From places I barely remember,
But somehow, still know.

They told me to forget.
To blend in.
To be nice.
To shrink.
To sit still while the fire in me screamed…
"WAKE UP."

Logan Of Love

# Chapter Six

The Game Masters are Weirdos Too

Let's be honest.

You keep waiting for some robe-wearing wizard to hand you a crystal, whisper in tongues, and tell you "You are ready, young one…"

But the truth is…

The ones writing the codes?

They're just as weird, wounded, and wildly wonderful as you.

They burp during meditation. They forget to ground themselves and then scream at the kettle. They get downloads while cleaning cat vomit off the floor.

You're not doing it wrong. You're just human.

This chapter is where the veil really thins, and you realise something wild:

There are no adults in the room.
There is no perfect version of you.
And the people who look like they have it all figured out? They're winging it, baby.

This is Divine Chaos with a Wi-Fi signal.

The Universe has always been messy, contradictory, and full of paradox. It grows wildflowers and volcanoes. It births both galaxies and gobshites.

So here's the cheat code:

Let go of the idea that you'll ever be fully ready.
Start where you are. With your full messy heart.

You don't need to cleanse your aura before you make a change.
You don't need to be healed to start healing others.
You don't need to be "high vibe" to be holy.
You are the glitch in the matrix that lets the light in.

Your weirdness? Your shadow? Your craving for snacks at 3AM?
That's data, darling. That's Divine.
The Game Masters made you quirky for a reason. It was your cosmic camouflage.

Scroll from the Universe:

Dusted off the bottom drawer of Andromeda… still sticky with stardust and spilled tea.

Dear Glitch in the Matrix,

You weren't sent to Earth to pretend to be perfect.
You were sent to remember your magic… through the mess.

You will not be initiated through titles.
You will be initiated through heartbreak.
Through loneliness.
Through rage that shakes your ribcage.
And Love that burns you clean.

The Game is not about escaping the pain.
It's about learning to dance with it.
To turn your grief into spells.
Your fear into fuel.
Your awkwardness into art.

Stop waiting to be picked.

Stop trying to tidy yourself up for their comfort.
You are the wild note in the choir.
The broken mirror that shows the truth.

If you've felt too weird to fit in, it's because you were built to break the pattern.

You are not the mistake.
You are the breaker of the cycle.

Signed,
The Game Masters (yes, even the one with the biscuits and Crocs)

Let Go of Perfect

Write down 3 ways you're still waiting to "be ready."
Burn it, bury it, or bin it. Buh-bye, illusions.

Bless the Mess

What was your last "WTF" moment? Journal it like a sacred scroll. Reframe it. What magic or lesson might have been hidden in the cat sick/chaos?

Divine Downloads in Dirty Dishes

Note a weird moment you felt guidance (even while hangry or hormonal).
Thank your guides. Even if they showed up in slippers and Crocs.

Holy Rage & Ribcage Rattles

When did you last feel wild emotion in your bones?
How did it initiate you? What did it burn clean?

Your Weird is Sacred

List 5 "weird" things about yourself.
Now rewrite each one as a superpower.

Stop Waiting to Be Picked

What dream, idea or expression are you postponing till you're

"better"?
Do one tiny messy step towards it today.

## *DoodleNotes*
### Your Sacred Space

# Chapter Seven

"Mirror Mirror, You Mad Bitch"
The real villain was always your reflection… but plot twist, she's also the bloody hero.

Let's get real:
Everyone talks about healing like it's bath bombs and playlists and sage smoke curling through your trauma like a cute Instagram filter.
But healing?
Nah babe, healing is ugly sobs, rage fits in the kitchen, overthinking your worth at 3:00 AM, and screaming into a pillow because you're tired of being the strong one.

But in that rawness… that's where the magic brews.

Because here's the cheat code:
Your triggers are your teachers.
Your reactions? They are treasure maps.
Your self-sabotage? A glitch in your matrix waiting to be hacked.

You wanna know why you keep meeting the same type of people, situations, heartbreaks, breakdowns?
Because the universe is yelling,
"Heal this shit so we can upgrade your timeline!"

And here's the twist no one tells you:
You can't fake healing.
You can't pretend to love yourself and still let people treat you like yesterday's leftovers.
You can't put glitter on your shadow and call it "enlightenment."

The Universe is WiFi-connected to your inner Bull. Shit.
It won't load new blessings on an old mindset.

So, you sit with yourself.
You hold the mirror up.
You stop avoiding the parts that scare you... the jealous one, the bitter one, the insecure one... and you say:

"Alright, roundtable. Let's heal this kingdom."

Because you're not here to be perfect.
You're here to be whole.

Scroll from the Universe:

Only visible in reflections, foggy windows, and those late-night stare-offs with yourself in the bathroom mirror.

Dear Shadow Walker,
You thought you were broken.
But you were breaking open.

Every jagged edge
Every crack in your soul
Was making room for your light to leak through.

The world told you to hide those parts.
To smooth them out.
But I... the Universe...
I wrote the codes into your wounds.

So look closer.
Inside your anger? Power.
Inside your guilt? Wisdom.
Inside your tears? The medicine.

You're not crazy, dramatic, or "too much."
You're a fucking oracle in training.
And your shadow isn't your enemy...
She's your oldest protector,

Your fiercest teacher,
Your key.

So stop trying to destroy her.
Sit beside her.
Listen.
Heal.
Integrate.

Because the world doesn't need another polished soul.
It needs one that remembers the dark and still chooses to glow anyway.

Signed,
The Universe, with a cracked mirror and mascara tears.

Look Yourself in the Eye (literally)
Stand in front of the mirror. No filter. No faking. Ask:
"What version of me am I pretending not to be today?"
Write it down.

Name the Villain:
What part of you is causing chaos right now?
Jealousy? Abandonment? Anger?
Give her a name. Let her speak.

Spot the Pattern, Break the Loop:
"Where am I reliving the same wound in a different costume?"
Track it. Write the scene. What's the lesson trying to break through?

Treasure Map Emotions:
Choose 1 trigger from this week.
Ask it:
"What are you trying to teach me?"
Let it answer through your pen.

Rage Ritual:
Safely release rage today.
Scream. Stomp. Write a "Fuck You" letter you don't send.
(Or DO... we're not judging)
Then:
What truth was buried beneath the fury?
Write it...

## DoodleNotes

### Your Sacred Space

# Chapter Eight

YOU'RE THE ARCHITECT, BABY

You've spent enough time decoding the matrix, now it's time to design your own realm within it.

You've cried through awakenings, laughed through breakdowns, saged the shite out of your home, and whispered affirmations while stirring your tea with a spoon that's seen war.

Now?

Now you claim your power and start being intentional about every freaking thing.

The Cheat Codes of Creation:

1. Words Are Wands.
If you're speaking like life's a slog, it will be. If you're moaning about what isn't, that's the only thing that grows. Speak like a spellcaster. Speak in outcomes, not worries.
Instead of "I don't want to be broke," say:
"I am aligned with opportunities and wealth finds me easily."

2. You Can't Fake Energy.
Vision boards don't work if your soul's rolling its eyes. You've got to feel the life you want in your bones. Dance like you're already living it. Make your choices like it's real now.

3. You Don't Chase… You Align.
Desperation is repellent. Sovereignty is magnetic. You don't "go after" … you become the frequency that draws it in.

Want Love? Be Love.
Want success? Embody worth.
Want peace? Start canceling subscriptions to chaos.

4. Expect It. Not Just Wish It.
The Universe isn't Santa Claus. It's more like Amazon Prime for your soul. You click 'order' by believing. You track it by aligning. You receive it by being present and open.

5. Decide Who You Are Every Day.
And show up like it's already coded into your cells. You can recalibrate any time… identity is malleable. Reality responds to who you're being, not what you're saying.

Scroll from the Universe:

Delivered through stardust and sass…

Dear Creator in Disguise,

I gave you a paintbrush and you've been using it like a fork.
Stop trying to understand the world… reimagine it.
Don't just read the rules… rewrite them.

Every thought you think is a command to the quantum soup.
Every word you speak echoes through dimensions.
Every feeling you feel is a signal, pulsing out like sonar to shape the field.

You are not a mistake.
You are not waiting for your moment.
You are the moment.
So don't ask me what to do next.
Ask yourself who you're becoming.

And remember… I'm not testing you.
I'm co-creating with you.
You are the spell.
You are the wand.
You are the fire.

Signed,
The Universe (and your Soul's Architect Hotline)

What are the top 3 things I've been unintentionally spellcasting into my life through my words?
How can I reword them into powerful affirmations that call in what I actually want?

"You Can't Fake Energy"
Where am I showing up with "meh" energy when my dreams need a full-body "hell yes"?
What would it look like to FEEL the future I want as if it's already mine today?

## DoodleNotes
### Your Sacred Space

# Chapter Nine

The Illusion of "Normal"

... And Why You Should Run From It Like It Owes You Soul Rent

Once upon a timeline, someone somewhere decided to call a cage a home,
a routine a life,
and mediocrity the dream.

And they named it "normal."
And everyone clapped.

But you? You were born allergic to it.
You were the child who side-eyed the system.
You asked why when they said because.
You asked what if when they said you can't.
You felt the glitch in the matrix, didn't you?

THE TRUTH THEY HIDE: NORMAL ISN'T SAFE... IT'S SEDATIVE.

They sell it like safety.
But it's sedation.

The 9–5–die plan.
The smile-and-nod culture.
The ghosting of your own joy because "that's just how life is."

It's a slow decay disguised as success.
A to-do list that never included your soul's desires.

Normal will have you ignoring your gut, betraying your truth, and calling it maturity.

## "NORMAL" IS A PROGRAM. YOU ARE THE GLITCH.

You came coded with something different.
A fire that doesn't negotiate.
A spirit that breaks through the static.

You're not broken.
You're the evidence that the old system is.

You don't "fit in" because your soul remembers stars while others chase status.
You feel too much because you were never meant to be numb.
You question everything because your DNA carries memory of truths buried beneath centuries of lies.

The ones who came before you?
Burned as witches.
Locked away as mad.
Laughed at for speaking to wind and dancing with their shadows.

But guess what?
They were us.
We're the return of the misfits,
the memory keepers,
the weird ones that make the Earth shake.

## SIGNS YOU'RE ESCAPING THE NORMAL TRAP

You feel heavy in spaces others thrive in.

You crave silence over small talk.

You ask "what's the point?" at jobs that others climb ladders in.

You cry when you feel truth, even if you can't explain it.

You know that Love isn't passive. It's a roar.

## SCROLL FROM THE UNIVERSE:

Dear Sacred Rulebreaker,

You are not too loud.
Your fire is just foreign to those who forgot they were born of it too.

You are not too sensitive.
You're just tuned into the frequency of reality beneath the illusion.

You are not lazy.
You just refuse to grind your soul into dust to build someone else's empire.

Let them measure their lives in salary slips and shoe sizes.
You'll be measuring yours in moments of ecstasy, epiphany, and evolution.

You are not late.
You are timeless.

You are not weird.
You are wonderfully wired differently… for a future only the brave can build.

You're not here to walk in their footsteps. You're here to burn a trail with bare feet and wild hair, holding truth like a torch.

So, drop the act.
Burn the blueprint.
Reclaim your wild.

They may call it chaos.
But we know…
it's freedom.

Signed,
The Universe (and your rulebreaker hero)

What parts of my life have I accepted as "normal" that actually drain my soul?

What beliefs, routines, or roles am I clinging to just because "that's how it's done"?

And what would my life look like if I replaced them with what feels true, alive, and wildly mine?

If I stopped trying to fit in and started fully showing up as myself… what would I say, do, create, or become?

What's the version of me that I've kept on mute to make others comfortable?

And what tiny (or massive) rebellion am I ready to take in her honour today?

# DoodleNotes
## Your Sacred Space

# Unfuck Your Fuck

## UNFUCK YOUR PROGRAMMING

Tonight, light a candle.
Not for calm.
But for rebellion.

Write the lies you've swallowed on scraps of paper:

"I have to be productive to be worthy."

"It's selfish to put myself first."

"I should just be grateful."

"This is just how life is."

Now burn those suckers.

And as the smoke rises, say this loud (or whisper it like a spell):

"I revoke all contracts made in fear. I return to my truth. I don't belong in a box... I build bonfires."

Then dance. Or cry. Or scream. Or smile.

That's the ritual.
That's the revolution.

Signed,
Your Higher Self (tattooed in stardust and dripping with truth)

## Chapter Ten

Why You Being "Too Much" Is the Exact Medicine the World Forgot it Needed

There's a wild, untamed rhythm in you.
It's messy. Loud. Fierce.
It doesn't ask for permission... and it bloody well shouldn't.

You've been told to tone it down, quiet your joy, dim your weird, compress your truth into something more "palatable."
More "pleasing."
More... acceptable.

But let's be honest... who has time to be a soggy digestive biscuit when you were born a galaxy-glazed donut with sprinkles of sacred rebellion?

Too much laughter?
You're the echo of joy in a world that forgot how to belly laugh.

Too many opinions?
You're the lightning bolt of clarity in conversations soaked in people-pleasing and vague nods.

Too sensitive?
You feel the undercurrents most people are numb to.
You read energy like ancient braille.

Too emotional?
Your tears are tidal scrolls, washing away what the world refuses to feel.

Your "too much" is your medicine.
And medicine doesn't always taste sweet. Sometimes it burns going down — but it heals.

The Universe didn't overfill your cup by accident... it filled it to overflowing because it knew you'd be the one brave enough to pour it out in all directions.

And yes, some will say it's "too intense."
They'll squirm. They'll avoid.
They'll project their own numbness onto your aliveness.

Let them.

Because you're not here to babysit other people's discomfort.
You're here to remember your fire.
And by standing fully, wildly, unapologetically in your "too-muchness,"
you give others the courage to unclench their own truth.

UNIVERSE SCROLL: "THE WILD ONES CODE"

To the ones who feel like hurricanes in a teacup...
You are not broken.
You are a mirror too clean for the world's dirt to hide.

Be loud. Be bright. Be sacred chaos.
You are not too much...
You are *exactly enough* to shake the foundations
of every false thing pretending to be truth.

So here's your reminder:
If someone tells you you're too much,
smile with your whole soul and whisper,
"Too much for what?"

Because medicine was never meant to be mild.

THE BOOK

## ✍ DoodleNotes

### Your Sacred Space

## *Chapter Eleven is the moment the game knows you're leveling up.*

Universal Mirror.... You are the Portal.

Cheat Code:
"11 is not just a number. it's a gateway. And the Key? you."

This is the sacred checkpoint.
The mirrored doorway.
The 11:11 moment.
Not just to see your reflection, but to remember that it's always been a two-way mirror...
You're not just observing the Universe.
You're also being observed by it.

And the question it's been waiting to ask you is:
"Are you ready to stop playing small?"

RITUAL: "The Portal Reflection"
(To activate your universal code)

Time: Do this under the moon or at 11:11 (AM or PM). Or whenever the fuck you want.
Tools: Mirror. Candle. Salt. Water. A pen. Your boldest truth. Or just you at 3am with anything laying around but you do need a morror.
Steps:

1. Light your candle or don't. Say:
"I call in the flame of truth, the reflection of all that I am and all that I'm becoming."

2. Gaze into the mirror. Not your face. Not your flaws. Your eyes. Deeper. See the soul, not the skin.

3. Sprinkle salt into the water. Stir clockwise or imagine it. Say: "I cleanse my perception. I reclaim my power."

4. Now whisper to your reflection something you've been afraid to admit. Something real.

5. Write it down or pop it into the notes on your phone. Then write the exact opposite as your affirmation.
Example:

"I've felt like I'm too much for people."

Affirmation: "I am the exact right medicine for those who are ready to rise."

6. Close your eyes and say:
"I step through the portal. I no longer shrink. I expand."

7. Snuff the candle. Keep the affirmation somewhere sacred.

8. Eat kale (jokes)

⚡ THE CHALLENGE: "Too Much Club" ⚡

For the next 11 days:
Say what you mean.
Wear what lights you up.
Laugh too loudly.
Say NO when your soul says no.
Say YES to what you'd normally "wait for the right time" to do.

And when someone says:

"You're a lot."
You look 'em in the eye and say:
"I know. It's called power."

Scroll from the Universe:
"My beloved chaos spark,
You've danced long enough with doubt.
Your fire isn't random.
Your truth isn't inconvenient.
You're the storm and the stillness.
The medicine that cracks the spell.
Walk tall, weird one.
The code was never meant to tame you—
It was meant to unlock you."

Signed,
The Universe (and your trusted Mirror probably wearing a party hat)




What truth am I ready to stop hiding from myself... no matter how messy, bold, or "too much" it feels?

What's one part of me I've dimmed to be digestible for others?
How would it feel to finally honour that part fully, loudly, unapologetically?

If 11:11 was a portal to my most powerful self... what version of me is waiting on the other side?

What does she/they/he look like, say, wear, create, demand, allow, refuse?
What's one choice I can make today to step into that version of me... like I'm already her?

## DoodleNotes
### Your Sacred Space

# Chapter Twelve

The Truth Isn't Always Polite (But It Is Always Freeing)

Scroll from the Universe
"Dear Wild One with Galaxies in Your Gaze,
Truth is not a weapon... it's a mirror.
It doesn't need to be wrapped in ribbons or softened for comfort.
You weren't sent here to dim or dilute; you were born to reveal.
Your voice shakes foundations because it speaks to souls, not egos.
When you open your mouth and truth flows out,
The ones meant for you will recognise the sound...
Like a long-lost melody they forgot they knew.
Keep speaking. Even when your voice trembles.
Even when the room goes silent.
Even when it costs you the comfort of the crowd.
You are not too much.
You are exact, precise, and necessary."

Reality Check
Truth isn't always nice.
It doesn't sit down with its legs crossed and whisper politely into napkins.
It's messy. It's loud. It arrives like a thunderclap and often leaves rubble behind.

But do you know what's built in that rubble?
Freedom. Real, wild, bone-deep freedom.

People will call you rude.
They'll say you're intense, overbearing, too direct.
They'll try to wrap their discomfort in your skin and make it your problem.
But here's the thing:
Your medicine was never meant to taste like sugar.

You're not here to win a popularity contest.
You're here to crack open cages with your voice and plant wildflowers in the ruins.
Let them flinch. Let them talk. Let them leave.
Your truth is too sacred to shrink.

Cheat Code:
"Silence isn't golden if it costs you your truth."
If you have to mute your essence to keep the peace,
Then it isn't peace... it's a prison.
Be honest. Be bold. Be unshakable in your knowing.
And remember: the ones who see you will never ask you to quiet your soul.


Universe says:
Some people need your truth like oxygen ... even if they gag at first breath.
You don't need to be liked by everyone, you need to be aligned with yourself.
So when you speak and it rattles someone?
Good. You've just struck a nerve worth waking up.
You're not here to be digestible...
You're here to be unforgettable.

Signed,
The Universe (and your "Let Them" Goddesses and Gods)

"What truths have I been silencing to keep others comfortable?"

Write freely. No filters. Whose peace have you been protecting at the cost of your own? What words have been simmering in your soul, begging to be released?

"If I let my truth speak without apology, what would it say today?"

Let it pour out. Imagine your truth as a thunderstorm or a wild poem. Don't water it down. Don't edit. Just write what your soul has been waiting to say.

## DoodleNotes
### Your Sacred Space

## Chapter Thirteen

The Final Glitch... Nothing Is Ever Really the End

Let's be clear. You're not done just because you reached the last chapter. The Universe doesn't work in straight lines... it loops, twists, spirals, and giggles while you try to make sense of it.

By now, you've learned to:

Call your power back like a boss

Laugh at your illusions

Reclaim your too-muchness as medicine

Flip fear the bird

Channel scrolls from the Universe like a wizard with Wi-Fi

But here's the final cheat code:

There is no final cheat code.

Because you are the game designer. You're writing code as you go... through the tears, the belly laughs, the messy mornings, the moonlit prayers, and the rogue snacks that weren't part of your spiritual plan but totally hit the spot anyway.

Here's the truth-bomb scroll from the Universe:

SCROLL FROM THE UNIVERSE
The Loop of Becoming

"You are not here to win.

You are not here to fix.
You are not here to impress.
You are here to remember.

To remember the divine glitch that is YOU.
To walk barefoot through chaos and still dance.
To love with reckless precision.
To say no when it's sacred.
To say yes when it's terrifying.

You are not broken.
You are not behind.
You are not late.

You are perfectly on time for your next becoming.
You will forget again.
That's okay.
You'll remember even deeper next time."

The Universe
(and probably your weird inner child with a glitter gun)

So, what now?

Now you live it.
You speak your truth like it's holy.
You rest like a revolution.
You laugh like it heals timelines (because it does).
You walk on, knowing the magic is not out there... it's in you, always has been.

And if you ever get lost again?

Read this book backwards.

We'll meet again in the spaces between your thoughts,
in the breath that slows your panic,
in the wind that reminds you... you were never alone.

Game on, soul traveler.

Signed,
The Universe and *Logan of Love* ❤

## "A Sprinkle of Stardust & Shenanigans"

Because every good spell (and book) ends with a giggle and gratitude.

## "With Love, Laughter & Cosmic Gratitude"

For all the souls who stayed up late with me chasing the stars.
(fear... False Evidence Appearing Real)

# The End That Never Was

This isn't the end,
not really at all,
just a breath between pages,
a pause in the call.

You wandered the lines
like a dreamer, now found,
unlocking the Magic
that's always been bound.

You broke the rules
with a wink and a grin,
you danced with your shadows,
and let the light back in.

Write on with your footsteps,
cast spells with your voice,
you are your own author
a power and choice.

When life feels too noisey,
when doubt starts to bite,


just open your palms...
you were born of starlight.

So go now, Beloved,
your story's begun...
The Book may be closing,
but you are the One.

# A Little Thank You

(because no epic cosmic journey is done alone... especially not one written at 3am in pyjamas with oat milk latte)

First off... if you're holding this book, thank you. You made it all the way through the madness, the magic, and the messiness that is The Book. You're a legend. Truly.

Now... this wouldn't exist without some very special souls who danced through the stars with me while I scribbled like a gremlin on a mission to decode the Universe.

Becky, my celestial co-pilot... thank you for seeing the Universe with me until the wee hours of the morning. You brought constellations to life and helped me crack codes only Grandmother Moon understood. Also, thanks for not judging our midnight Schweet Treat choices. We wandered galaxies and still made it back in time for breakfast. You're forever my fellow Soul-Sis-Star stargazer.

Zaria, your guidance was like a spiritual sat nav... always rerouting me back to truth, even when I took several (okay, many) dramatic detours.

❤ Rab... my husband, my anchor, my friend... thank you for your unwavering support, your love, and for pretending to understand what I meant when I said "I've just been quantum leaping with Grandmother Spider."

Natalie, Bobby & Graham... my beautiful wildlings. Thank you for being your brilliant, chaotic, magical selves. You each helped me see the world in new ways. You are my biggest teachers (and occasional gremlins, let's be honest).

Little AJ… thank you for bringing a blast of light into our family. You are joy wrapped in a tiny, cheeky package.

Kate… you listened. Really listened. And that is a rare kind of magic. Thank you for supporting me even when I made no sense whatsoever and said things like "I think the crow has a message."

And to every soul who has ever asked, "Is it just me, or is this life thing a bit weird?"… this book was written for you.

And to Moon & Me, my moon tribe, my soul-sisters and brothers and fellow weirdlings… you were the cosmic mirror I didn't know I needed. This book wouldn't exist without your presence, power, and permission to be exactly who I am. You helped me turn healing into a homecoming.

Thank you all for being part of this wild, wondrous ride. The Universe wrote this book… I just held the pen.

Now go sparkle. And remember… the cheat codes were inside you all along

Stay messy, stay magical, and never stop asking the wild questions.

With all my Love,
*Logan of Love*

Printed in Great Britain
by Amazon

c21167b5-56b9-4449-8bb7-94a5108e6facR01